FRESHFLAVORS
fromISRAEL

First Published in Israel in 2008 by Al Hashulchan Gastronomic Media Ltd.,
36 Ashkenazi St., Tel Aviv 61131 Israel

All recipes are kosher.

ISBN 978-965-7279-03-8

www.hashulchan.co.il

Translation and Research: Janna Gur, Rami Hann
Copy Editor: Frances Zetland
Design: Varda Amir, Anna Shapiro
Production Manager: Iris Gelbert

Photography
Danya Wiener — 8, 11, 16, 19, 21, 30, 32, 33, 51, 58, 59, 68, 81, 85, 87, 95, 99, 107, 108,
115, 117, 122, 129, 131
Eilon Paz — 12, 23, 40, 41, 42, 43, 45, 47, 48, 70, 79, 80, 92, 100, 101, 102, 103, 116, 121,
135
Daniel Layla — 15, 37, 57, 61, 65, 66, 67, 72, 73, 74, 75, 76, 81, 96, 97, 110, 111, 132, 134,
136, 137
Rian — 28, 29, 54, 118, 119
Ronen Mangan — 34, 93, 124, 125, 127
Michal Lehnart — 53, 82, 83
Michal Revivo — 105

Food Styling
Rotem Nir — 34, 68, 93, 117, 118, 119, 124, 125, 127
Talia Gon Asif — 16, 21, 51, 58, 59, 81, 95, 122
Dalit Russo — 8, 11, 19, 24, 87, 115, 129, 131

The following recipes are reproduced with permission from
Shavuot, Israeli Celebration 2008
published by **Tnuva Dairies:**
Fatoush Salad with Labane Cheese (p. 20)
Shakshuka with Eggplants and Goat Cheese (p. 50)
Couscous Salad with Chickpeas, Raisins and Feta Cheese (p. 80)
Stuffed Pepper Schnitzel (p. 59)
Eggplant Soup with Feta, Mint and Sumac (p. 94)
Cheesecake with Assorted Nuts (p. 123)

FRESHFLAVORS
from ISRAEL

Ruth Oliver, Orly Pely-Bronshtein,
Shaily Lipa-Angel

Edited by Janna Gur

Al Hashulchan
Gastronomic Media

Contents

Family Dinners 62

The Festive Table 88

Something Sweet 112

MEZE & SALADS

Tahini Dip

The more we use tahini the more enamored we become with this magical sesame paste. Start with the basic dip and go on to discover how it can be used to upgrade antipasti (p. 10), to give a velvety touch to a ceviche (p. 10), and even as the basis for delicious cookies or ice cream (p. 128, p. 130) The key to a successful tahini dish is choosing top-grade raw tahini. Taste it straight from the jar — it should have a smooth, nutty, slightly sweet flavor.

Ingredients (serves 4-6)
1 cup top quality raw tahini
1-2 tablespoons freshly squeezed lemon juice
2-3 cloves garlic, crushed (optional)
Salt to taste

Whisk all the ingredients in a large bowl and gradually add ice-cold water. Don't be alarmed when the first bit of water makes the paste thick and lumpy. Keep whisking and adding liquid and the mixture will get thinner and silky smooth. The amount of water depends on the desired consistency: 1/2 cup for a thick tahini dip, 1 cup or even a bit more for a thin sauce suitable for pouring over vegetables or falafel.

Green Tahini Dip Add 1/2 cup parsley, 1/4 cup coriander and 1/4 cup mint, all chopped, to the basic tahini dip recipe.
Nutty Tahini Dip Add 1/2 cup coarsely ground pistachio nuts or walnuts to the basic tahini dip recipe.

Four Ways with Tahini:
1. Pour tahini dip over Israeli Salad (p. 13)
2. Mix equal amounts of raw tahini and plain yogurt and serve with stuffed or roasted vegetables.
3. Pour raw tahini or prepared dip over fried or grilled fish fillets, kebabs or meat patties.
4. Mix raw tahini with honey (or better still silan, date honey, see p. 92). Serve with nuts and dried dates.

Ceviche with Beetroot and Tahini

The acidity of fish cured in lemon juice welcomes the smooth and nutty tahini and blends beautifully with the sweetness of beetroots. A charmingly different take on the popular South American delicacy.

Ingredients (serves 4)
500 g (1 lb) of fresh, firm-fleshed saltwater fish (greater amberjack, sea bream, etc.)
2 beetroots, cooked, peeled and cubed
1 spring onion, chopped
1/4 cup raw tahini
3 tablespoons freshly squeezed lemon juice
3 tablespoons olive oil
3 tablespoons fresh coriander leaves, chopped

Mix the ingredients and serve at once, or let stand for 5-10 minutes for a stronger lemony taste.

Roasted Vegetable Antipasti with Tahini Sauce

This is one of those recipes whose end result is greater than the sum of its simple ingredients. A tiny amount of sugar is used to caramelize the veggies.

Ingredients (serves 4)
2 bunches of spring onions, or 4 small sweet potatoes quartered lengthwise, or 2 whole leeks
Kosher salt
Olive oil
2 cloves garlic, sliced
3 sprigs thyme
A pinch of brown sugar (optional)
To serve:
1/2 cup raw tahini

1. Preheat the oven to 200°C (400°F).
2. Arrange the vegetables on a baking tray lined with baking paper. Season with salt and sugar, drizzle on some olive oil and top with garlic and thyme.
3. Put the tray in the oven and reduce the temperature to 150°C (300°F). Roast until tender and slightly brown (5 minutes for onions, 10 for leeks, 15 for sweet potatoes).
4. Remove from the oven, pour the tahini over the hot vegetables and serve at once.

Variation For a more subtle taste use prepared tahini dip (p. 9) instead of raw tahini.

The Israeli Salad

Next to scrambled eggs in the morning, stuffed in a pita together with shawarma or falafel for a quick lunch, topped with tahini or cottage cheese for a light supper, Israelis must have their salad at least once a day. Preparation is easy. Just make sure you use fresh flavorful vegetables at room temperature (refrigeration dulls their flavor), chop them with a sharp knife to avoid crushing, and serve at once.

Ingredients (serves 2-4)

1 juicy lemon, halved
4 firm ripe tomatoes, diced
4 unpeeled cucumbers, diced
1 red onion, finely diced
1 sweet red pepper, seeded and diced
1 clove garlic, crushed
1/2 fresh hot green pepper, seeded and chopped (optional)
Dash cinnamon
1 teaspoon sumac (optional)
Salt and freshly ground black pepper to taste
3 tablespoons extra virgin olive oil
2-3 tablespoons parsley and/or coriander and/or mint leaves, chopped

1. Squeeze the juice of half the lemon. Remove the pips from the remaining half and peel the skin (including the white pulp). Chop finely.
2. Place the chopped lemon and the lemon juice in a bowl, add the remaining ingredients and toss. Taste and adjust the seasoning. Serve immediately.

Variation To make your salad even more wholesome add coarsely grated carrots, finely sliced cabbage (red or white), chopped young radishes, fennel bulbs, spring onions and chives.

Savory Granola

Sweet and crunchy, served with yogurt and fresh fruit, granola is perfect morning fare. Orly Pely-Bronshtein, cookbook author and senior food editor at Al Hashulchan Magazine, came up with the idea of a savory version that goes hand-in-hand with our favorite morning treat — the chopped salad.

Ingredients (makes about 500 g/1 lb)
21/2 cups rolled oats (not instant)
Dash olive oil (optional)
3 tablespoons sesame seeds
3 tablespoons sunflower seeds
3 tablespoons pumpkin seeds
1/2 cup pecans
1 teaspoon coriander seeds
1 teaspoon whole cumin seeds
1 tablespoon paprika
1/2 teaspoon salt
5 sun-dried tomatoes, chopped

1. Heat a non-stick pan (with a little olive oil, if you are using it) and toast the oats for 2-3 minutes. Remove from the pan using a slotted spoon and cool.
2. In the same pan, toast separately until golden the sesame seeds, sunflower seeds, pumpkin seeds, pecans and whole spices.
3. Cool and mix with paprika and sun-dried tomatoes.
4. Store in an airtight jar up to 2 months.

Serving suggestion Put freshly chopped Israeli salad (p. 13) in a bowl, pour on some yogurt, and sprinkle generously with savory granola. Serve at once.

Labane — Yogurt Cheese

Sour tasting and creamy, labane is the easiest cheese to make at home. Sheep milk yogurt makes an especially good labane. Cow milk yogurt is also good.

Ingredients
5-6 cups yogurt, preferably sheep milk (at least 3% fat)
2 teaspoons salt
Olive oil
Za'atar spice mix (p. 20)

1. Mix the yogurt with the salt and pour into the center of a clean cheesecloth. Tie the corners together to form a sack.
2. Hang the sack over the sink or a bowl and let the liquid drain for 24 hours. Hang over a bowl in the refrigerator for another 24 hours or more until it reaches the desired consistency.
3. Transfer to a jar and cover with olive oil. Seal tightly.
4. **To serve:** Spread on a plate, pour over some olive oil and sprinkle with za'atar.

Labane Balls
in Chili-flavored Oil

A particularly attractive way to store and serve labane cheese.

Ingredients (makes about 30 balls)
3 cups labane cheese (p. 17)
2-3 cups extra virgin olive oil
1 heaping tablespoon chili flakes

1. Pour the oil into a glass jar, add chili and mix thoroughly.
2. Roll the cheese into balls the size of small apricots and place them carefully in the jar, one at a time. Make sure the oil completely covers the balls. Close the jar. Store in a cool dark place for up to several months.

Fatoush Salad with Labane

Take vegetable salad, add some toasted pita and you have fatoush — a much loved Middle Eastern salad . Add some labane and you have a complete summer meal in one bowl — delicious and filling.

Ingredients (serves 4)

1 pita bread
Olive oil for brushing
30 cherry tomatoes, halved
10 radishes, quartered
3 cucumbers cut into 1 cm (1/2 inch) cubes
1 red onion, halved and thinly sliced
2 tablespoons freshly squeezed lemon juice
1 teaspoon natural vinegar
Salt and freshly ground black pepper
1 cup labane cheese (p. 17)
1 teaspoon za'atar spice mix (see below)

1. Preheat the oven to 200°C (400°F).
2. Halve the pita into 2 discs and brush each one with olive oil. Cut each disc into 8 triangular wedges. Arrange on a baking sheet lined with baking paper and bake for 8-10 minutes until golden and crisp. Let cool.
3. Mix the rest of the ingredients except the labane and the za'atar spice mix, and season to taste.
4. Put a nice dollop of labane on each pita wedge, sprinkle on some za'atar and a drop of olive oil, and serve on top of the salad.

Za'atar Spice Mix

Za'atar (Arabic for hyssop) is a Middle Eastern spice mixture based on wild oregano, a plant similar to hyssop (Biblical *eizov*). Wild oregano, also known as white oregano or Lebanese oregano, is a rare protected plant and commercial za'atar often substitutes it with hyssop, oregano or thyme, or a combination of the three. Za'atar is sprinkled on hummus, labane and vegetable salads and used in marinades for fish and chicken.

Ingredients

2 tablespoons sesame seeds
1 tablespoon sumac
1/2 cup dried hyssop and/or oregano
1/2 teaspoon salt

1. Toast the sesame seeds in a dry skillet until golden.
2. Grind the dried hyssop or oregano with a mortar and pestle or in a food processor. Mix with the sesame and sumac and season with salt. Keep in an airtight jar.

Za'atar Spread Add 2/3 cup olive oil and grated rind and juice of one lemon.

Cherry Tomatoes with Coriander and Lemon

Easy to make, juicy and crunchy at the same time. Make sure you serve enough bread or pita to mop up the delicious juices left at the bottom of the bowl.

Ingredients (serves 4)

3 cups cherry tomatoes, washed and halved
1/2 cup coriander leaves, chopped
1/2 cup pine nuts, toasted
2 tablespoons lemon juice
1 teaspoon grated lemon rind
3 tablespoons aromatic extra virgin olive oil
Salt and freshly ground black pepper to taste

Toss all ingredients together in a large bowl and serve immediately.

Variations

Add 1 tablespoon raw tahini.
Sprinkle with some crumbled feta cheese.

Beetroot and Pomegranate Salad

Erez Komarovsky, Erez's Galilee Cooking School, Matat

Deep purple of the beetroot, garnet red of the pomegranate seeds and bright green of the coriander leaves. This salad is as flavorful as it is beautiful.

Ingredients (serves 6)

3-4 medium beetroots
2 tablespoons pomegranate concentrate
2-3 tablespoons freshly squeezed lemon juice
1-2 dried chili peppers, crushed
Coarse sea salt
1/4 cup delicate olive oil
1/2 cup fresh coriander leaves
1 cup pomegranate seeds

1. Boil the beetroots in water until tender. Cool, peel and cut into very small dice.
2. Mix with the pomegranate concentrate, lemon juice, peppers and coarse sea salt. Set aside for about 15 minutes.
3. Mix the salad with the coriander leaves and pomegranate seeds, pour the olive oil on top and serve.

Flame-Roasting Eggplants

Eggplants roasted on an open flame are the starting point for innumerable dishes — from spreads and salads to soups and pastry. The process can be a bit messy but is definitely worth the effort as the smoky aroma adds immensely to the taste.

First line your stovetop with aluminum foil. Place a whole eggplant (or more than one if you are confident) on a rack over the open flame and roast, turning occasionally, until the skin is scorched and blackened and the flesh feels soft when pierced with a wooden skewer or a fork. Cool slightly and peel, carefully removing every last bit of scorched skin, or cut in half lengthwise and scoop out the flesh with a wooden spoon.

Ideally, roasted eggplant should be served shortly after roasting and seasoned while still warm. But if you need to store it for later, drain the roasted flesh of excess liquid, cover with oil and refrigerate. Season before serving.

5 Ways
with Roasted Eggplants

1. Roasted Eggplant with Tahini
Add 1/2 cup raw tahini seasoned with 3-4 tablespoons lemon juice, 2 cloves crushed garlic, 2-3 tablespoons chopped parsley, a pinch of salt and freshly ground black pepper to the flesh of two roasted eggplants. If the mixture is too thick, add water gradually and stir to desired consistency. Sprinkle with toasted pine nuts before serving.

2. Roasted Eggplant with Pecans and Blue Cheese
Add about 1/2 cup crumbled blue (Roquefort style) cheese and 1/2 cup toasted chopped pecans to the flesh of two roasted eggplants.

3. Romanian-style Roasted Eggplant Salad
Add 1/2 cup oil, 3 cloves crushed garlic, salt and freshly ground black pepper to the flesh of two roasted eggplants. You may also add two grated onions and 2 peeled, grated tomatoes.

4. Roasted Eggplant and Goat Cheese Mousse
Whisk 1 cup of soft goat cheese with 1/4 cup whipping cream and combine with the chopped flesh of 3 flame-roasted eggplants. Whip 3/4 cup of whipping cream to soft peaks, fold in the eggplant mixture and season with salt, pepper and a dash of Tabasco. Serve on toasts.

5. Whole Roasted Eggplant Entrée
Cut open slightly cooled roasted eggplants, taking care to keep them whole. Place one eggplant on each serving plate. Pour small puddles of raw tahini, olive oil and lemon juice on the flesh of the eggplants. Season with salt and pepper and garnish with fresh herbs (oregano, hyssop, thyme, etc.) and serve at once. You may also add silan (date honey, see p. 92) or seeds and flesh of fresh ripe tomatoes.

2 More Ways with Roasted Eggplants
1. Prepare delicious eggplant soup, that can be served chilled or warm. See recipe on page 94.
2. Use roasted eggplant to make filling for crispy bourekitas. See recipe on page 111.

Cantaloupe
and Carrot Salad

**Erez Komarovsky, Erez's Galilee Cooking
School, Matat**

One is a fruit, the other a vegetable. One is
soft and luscious, the other hard and crunchy.
Both are bright orange and go surprisingly well
together.

Ingredients (serves 3-4)
Half a cantaloupe
2 carrots
3 tablespoons freshly squeezed lemon juice
1 tablespoon silan (date honey, see p. 92)
or 3/4 tablespoon honey
1/2 cup mint leaves
4 tablespoon pine nuts

1. Slice the melon very thin. Slice the carrots
using a cucumber peeler.
2. Mix silan (or honey) with lemon juice and
pour over the carrot and cantaloupe. Toss with
mint leaves.
3. Lightly toast the pine nuts and sprinkle on
top. Serve at once.

Orange and Olive Salad

Chef Guy Peretz, Culinary Consultant

The tangy sweetness of oranges, the piquant saltiness of olives, the cool aroma of coriander leaves, and a fiery touch of harissa: this is one of the most tempting offerings on the Moroccan Jewish meze table. The taste only gets better overnight so it's perfect for making ahead.

Ingredients (serves 4-6)

50 g (2 oz) dried black olives, halved and pitted
1 orange, peeled and diced
1 tablespoon harissa (p. 32)
1 tablespoon fresh coriander leaves, chopped
1/2 teaspoon cumin
1/4 cup freshly squeezed lemon juice
3 tablespoons olive oil
5 cloves garlic, chopped

Combine the ingredients and let stand for at least 2 hours, preferably overnight, in the refrigerator. Serve at room temperature.

Harissa

Fairly piquant but nowhere near as hot as Yemenite zhug, this condiment is a great enhancer of any sandwich and many kinds of salads.

Ingredients (makes 2 cups)
1/2 kg (1 lb) dried sweet red peppers
2-3 dried hot red peppers
10 cloves garlic
1/2 cup olive oil
1 tablespoon salt
1 tablespoon ground cumin
Juice of 2 lemons

1. Grind the dried peppers and the garlic with a mortar and pestle or in a meat grinder . A blender may be used as well, but will produce a more liquid harissa.
2. Stir in the olive oil, salt, cumin and lemon juice. Taste and adjust the seasoning.

Variation Grind some fresh parsley or fresh coriander together with the peppers and garlic.

Watermelon Cubes with Salty Cheese and Capers

Nobody really knows the origin of the watermelon-and-salty cheese combination, but over the years it has become an Israeli culinary staple. Like cheese and fruit at the end of an elegant French dinner, this surprising sweet-and-savory match makes a delightfully refreshing finale to a heavy meal, or a lovely summer afternoon snack. The following recipe offers a gourmet twist to this local favorite.

Ingredients (makes 25 cubes)
1 watermelon
3/4 cup brinza or feta cheese, crumbled
1/4 cup walnuts, roasted and chopped coarsely
Black pepper, ground coarsely
Pickled capers

1. Cut the watermelon into 5 cm (2 inch) cubes. Using a melon baller, scoop the flesh out of the topside of each cube.
2. Mix the cheese and walnuts and season with the coarsely ground black pepper.
3. Fill the watermelon cubes with the cheese and walnut mixture and garnish with the capers. Arrange on a tray and serve.

Tomato and Peach Gazpacho

Chef Oren Luxemburg, Bariba, Tel Aviv

It should come as no surprise that a nation so crazy about vegetable salads would fall in love with this chilled Spanish soup, which can be described as liquid salad. Tomatoes, cucumbers, peppers and onions are all there, along with olive oil and parsley. The surprising addition of peaches adds a lovely taste to this ultimate summertime chiller.

Ingredients (serves 12)

3 slices of whole wheat bread, without the crust
1 kg (2 lbs 4 oz) ripe tomatoes, peeled, seeded and cut in chunks
2 cucumbers, cut in chunks
1 red bell pepper, seeded and cut in chunks
1 kg (2 lbs 4 oz) ripe peaches, peeled and cut in chunks
1 red onion, cut in chunks
2 cloves garlic, crushed
4 cups mineral water
4 cups tomato juice
1/3 cup dry red wine
1 large bunch parsley
1/3 cup freshly squeezed lemon juice
2 tablespoons brown sugar
2 teaspoons fine salt
1 teaspoon freshly ground black pepper

To serve:

1/2 cup extra virgin olive oil
1 bunch baby greens or micro greens

1. Soak the bread in one cup of water, drain and squeeze out the liquid.
2. Purée all the ingredients except the olive oil in a food processor until smooth. For a finer smoother consistency, pass the gazpacho through a fine sieve. Taste and adjust the seasoning.
3. Refrigerate at least two hours, preferably overnight.
4. Pour into bowls or glasses, drizzle with olive oil and garnish with greens.

LUNCH ON THE GO

Falafel

It may have lost its supremacy to shawarma and sabich as the king of Israeli street food, but falafel is still going strong. Easily made at home, it is great stuffed in a pita or served on a plate with hummus or tahini.

Ingredients (makes 10-12 generous servings)
1 kg (2 lb 4 oz) dry chickpeas soaked in water overnight
1 large onion
2/3 cup garlic cloves, peeled
1/2 cup fresh parsley, coarsely chopped
1/2 cup fresh coriander, coarsely chopped
1 teaspoon toasted coriander seeds
5-6 Shipka peppers (small hot green pickled peppers) or 1/2-1 teaspoon dried hot red pepper
11/4 tablespoons ground cumin
Pinch of ground cardamom
1 tablespoon salt
1 teaspoon freshly ground black pepper
1 level teaspoon baking powder
2 tablespoons flour
1 level tablespoon baking soda

4-5 tablespoons water
Oil for deep-frying
To Serve:
Oven-fresh pita
Tahini dip (p. 9)
Hummus dip (p. 44)
Vegetable salad (p. 13)

1. Drain the soaked chickpeas and rinse thoroughly. Grind them with the onion, garlic, parsley, coriander and Shipka peppers (or the dry hot red pepper) in a meat grinder or food processor, but do not purée; a slightly coarse consistency makes crunchier falafels. Season with cumin, cardamom, salt and black pepper. Add the baking powder and flour, mix well and refrigerate for one hour.
2. Before frying, dissolve the baking soda in 4-5 tablespoons water, add to the batter and mix well.
3. Moisten a falafel tool or ice cream scoop and form falafel patties, or roll walnut-size balls with moist hands.
4. Heat the oil for deep-frying to medium heat. Oil that is too hot will brown the falafels on the outside and leave the inside uncooked. Check the temperature by test-frying one ball. Fry in small batches on both sides, 4-5 minutes, until the balls turn golden-brown. Remove with a slotted spoon and drain the excess oil in a colander.
5. Serve promptly in a pita, spread with hummus dip. Add some vegetable salad and drip tahini on top.

Green Falafel Add one more cup of chopped parsley and coriander and grind with the rest of the ingredients..
Extra-crunchy Falafel Dip the balls in sesame seeds before frying.

Sabich

Sabich, one of the most popular local sandwich combos, is actually the name of a gentleman of Iraqi origin who owned a small kiosk in the town of Ramat-Gan. Sabich did not invent anything. All he did was combine some of the foods enjoyed by Iraqi Jews following Saturday morning services at synagogue, stuff it all into a pita, and offer it to the general public. Today, sabich is served even in classy cafés, where focaccia or sourdough bread replace the pita but the filling remains the same.

Ingredients
Thin eggplant slices, salted, drained and washed
Oil for deep-frying
Hard-boiled eggs, sliced (preferably brown)
Amba (Iraqi mango chutney)
Hummus spread (p. 44) or tahini dip (p. 9)
Fresh pita

1. Deep-fry the eggplant slices until dark brown. Remove from the oil, drain, and thoroughly soak up the excess oil with paper towel.
2. Spread tahini or hummus on the inside of a pita, stuff with fried eggplant slices and sliced hard-boiled egg, drip some amba on top and enjoy!

Recommended extras Finely diced vegetable salad (p. 13), tomato wedges, diced pickled cucumbers, onion slices, chopped parsley, slices of boiled potatoes.

Amba Bright yellow, hot and aromatic, Iraqi amba may be hard to find outside of Israel. It can be substituted by harissa (p. 32) or another hot condiment. Indian mango chutney is an option, as long as it is spicy.

Brown Eggs You can use plain hard-boiled eggs, but the real sabich requires this nutty tasting, mahogany-colored Iraqi specialty. Preparation is easy: line a wide pot with a thick layer of onion skins (you'll need plenty — the greengrocer should give them to you for nothing), hang a couple of tea bags inside the pot, arrange the eggs on the onion skins, pour hot water to cover, season with salt and pepper, and cook uncovered for an hour. Use an old pot because the skins and the tea will color the metal.

Hummus

Originally a Middle Eastern breakfast dish, hummus is consumed in Israel throughout the day and enjoys the status of the national dish. The best hummus is served at Hummusiya joints, but wonderful fresh hummus can be easily made at home. All you need is top quality raw tahini, soaked and cooked chickpeas, and a few basic spices.

Basic Hummus Dip

Ingredients (serves 8-10)
1/2 kg (1 lb 2 oz) small dry chickpeas
1 tablespoon + 1/2 teaspoon baking soda
1 cup raw top quality tahini
1 tablespoon freshly squeezed lemon juice
2 cloves garlic, crushed
Salt to taste

1. Soak the chickpeas overnight in a large bowl of cold water with one tablespoon of baking soda.
2. Drain and rinse the chickpeas and put them in a large pan. Add water until it reaches 2-3 cm (1 inch) above the chickpeas. Add the remaining 1/2 teaspoon of baking soda and bring to a boil. Cook covered over low heat for 2-3 hours, until the chickpeas are very soft. Cool slightly, drain and save some of the cooking liquid.
3. Put the chickpeas in a food processor, add 2/3 cup of the tahini and process until almost smooth. If the paste is too thick, add a few tablespoons of the cooking liquid. Season with lemon, garlic and salt; taste and adjust the seasoning. For a richer creamier version, add the remaining tahini and process until the hummus is completely smooth and fluffy.

Galilee Style Hummus Set aside 1 cup of cooked chickpeas. Purée the rest with 1/2 cup of raw tahini and the seasonings. Add the whole chickpeas and mix, slightly mashing the chickpeas. The texture should remain somewhat chunky.

To make ahead Soak and cook the chickpeas, put in small containers together with some of the cooking liquid and freeze. When ready to serve, defrost in the microwave and follow the recipe (step 3).

A Perfect Hummus Plate

This is the way hummus would be served in a real hummusiya. The spicy sauce will keep for a long time so make a large amount and store in an airtight jar in a cool dark place.

Ingredients (serves 6-8)
Basic hummus dip (see recipe on p. 44)
The Sauce:
1 cup freshly squeezed lemon juice
2 teaspoons ground cumin
1 teaspoon salt
1 teaspoon hot red pepper, chopped
1 tablespoon garlic, crushed
4-5 Shipka peppers (small hot green pickled peppers), seeded and chopped
To Serve:
Raw tahini
Olive oil
Chopped fresh parsley
Chopped onion

1. Mix the ingredients for the sauce and set aside for one hour.
2. Spoon 2-3 heaping tablespoons of hummus dip onto each plate and spread around the rim, leaving a crater in the center. Fill the crater with one tablespoon of raw tahini. Pour over 2-3 tablespoons of the sauce, drizzle with some olive oil and sprinkle chopped parsley and onion.

Hummus with Whole Chickpeas Add 2-3 tablespoons of warm cooked chickpeas to each plate of hummus dip. Pour the sauce and the olive oil on top and serve with chopped parsley and onion.

Hummus with Meat and Pine Nuts
Chef Avi Steinitz

Offered in many hummus eateries, this meal on one plate is delicious and filling.

Ingredients (serves 4-6)
600 g (1 1/2 lb) basic hummus dip (p. 44)
The Meat:
4 tablespoons olive oil
450 g (1 lb) beef ground with 100 g (3 1/2 oz) lamb fat
1 large onion, finely chopped
3 cloves garlic, finely chopped
Salt and freshly ground black pepper
3/4 teaspoon baharat spice mix (p. 83)
Dash of ground chili pepper
2/3 cup parsley, chopped
2-3 tablespoons pine nuts, lightly toasted

1. Heat the oil in a large, heavy, hot skillet and fry the onions until they turn golden. Add the meat and stir-fry for 2-3 minutes, breaking it down into small crumbs with a fork. Add garlic, season with salt, pepper and baharat and fry 1-2 minutes. Add half the parsley, mix well and remove from the stove. Keep warm.
2. Spoon the hummus onto plates and spread around the rim, leaving a crater in the center. Heap the meat mixture in the crater, sprinkle with the remaining parsley and top with pine nuts. Drizzle some olive oil and serve at once.

Variation If you don't like the aroma of lamb or can't get lamb fat, use only beef. Make sure it has a relatively high fat content or the mixture will be too dry.

Pickled (Moroccan) Lemons

A wonderfully versatile addition to your kitchen pantry: for sandwiches, salads and marinades.

Tunisian Sandwich

Here is yet another ethnic delicacy that has become an all-Israeli favorite. Originally the sandwich was served in a fricasse — a Tunisian deep-fried roll. Today, lighter and more readily available breads are preferred, usually baguette or ciabatta rolls.

Ingredients (makes 4 sandwiches)
4 bread rolls (baguette or ciabatta)
Hot condiment (e.g. harissa, p. 32)
2 small cans (160 grams, 6 oz) tuna in oil, drained
2 boiled potatoes, peeled and sliced
4 hard-boiled eggs, sliced lengthwise
4 tablespoons black olives, pitted
4 tablespoons pickled lemons, coarsely chopped (see recipe on this page)
4 teaspoons pickled capers, chopped

Cut each roll lengthwise. Spread with hot sauce and fill with tuna fish, potato slices and hard-boiled egg slices. Add one tablespoon each of olives, pickled lemons and chopped capers. Serve promptly.

Variations Spread the roll with hummus dip, tahini or mayonnaise before assembling the sandwich. Add pickled cucumber slices and/or finely diced vegetable salad.

Ingredients
1 kg (2 lb 4 oz) yellow-skinned lemons, sliced thinly or cut into small wedges, pips removed
Kosher salt
5 cloves garlic
2 small hot peppers, red or green
4-6 allspice berries
4 bay leaves
Sweet and/or hot paprika
Freshly squeezed lemon juice, to cover
Oil, to seal

1. Dip the lemon slices in the salt and arrange them in layers in a sterilized glass jar. Place garlic cloves, whole peppers, bay leaves and allspice berries between the layers of lemon. Press down hard until juice begins to run out. Pour the lemon juice on top. Seal by covering it with a generous layer of oil.
2. Close the lid and keep in the refrigerator for 3 months. When the curing process has been completed, discard the garlic, allspice, peppers and bay leaves.

Pickled Lemon Spread Purée the pickled lemons in a food processor to a smooth paste, transfer to sterilized jars and seal with olive oil. This spread will keep refrigerated for many months.

Shakshuka with Eggplant and Goat Cheese

Fiery red with puddles of white and yellow, this colorful piquant dish is eaten directly from the pan. A thick slice of fresh bread to mop up the spicy sauce is a must. Basic shakshuka has two compulsory ingredients — tomatoes and eggs — but this is only a beginning. The following version, enhanced with fried eggplant cubes and soft goat cheese, is one of our favorites.

Ingredients (serves 6)
1/4 cup + 3 tablespoons olive oil
1 medium eggplant diced into 1 cm (1/2 inch) cubes
2 cloves garlic, sliced
8 ripe tomatoes cut into 2 cm (1 inch) cubes
1/2 teaspoon ground cumin
1 teaspoon hot and/or sweet paprika
Salt and freshly ground black pepper
6 eggs
4-5 slices fresh soft goat cheese

1. Heat 1/4 cup of the oil in a large, deep skillet over medium-high heat and sauté the eggplant until golden. Remove and set on paper towel to absorb the excess oil.
2. Lower the heat and add the 3 tablespoons of oil. Add the garlic and sauté for half a minute, taking care not to let it get brown. Add the tomatoes and eggplants, season with cumin, salt, pepper and paprika, and cook uncovered for 10 minutes. Taste and adjust the seasoning. The sauce must be flavorful and fully seasoned before adding the eggs.
3. Break the eggs, one by one, into a small bowl and slide them carefully into the frying pan. Arrange the cheese slices on top, cover and cook for 2-5 minutes (depending on how you like your eggs). Serve at once with lots of fresh bread or challah.

Eija — Omelet with Herbs

This local answer to the French *omelette aux fines herbes* is one of Israel's favorite street snacks. It is piquant, tasty, and goes well with any kind of bread, but is best when stuffed in a pita with tahini and hot sauce.

Ingredients (serves 2-3)
4 eggs
Oil for frying
1/2 onion, sliced
1 cup herbs (parsley, dill, spearmint, coriander), chopped
2 spring onions, chopped
Salt and white pepper
1 tablespoon matzo flour or breadcrumbs (optional)

1. Heat a non-stick pan, add a little oil and brown the onions.
2. In the meantime, beat the eggs with the herbs, spring onions, salt, pepper and breadcrumbs.
3. Pour the egg mixture into the pan and lower the heat. Fry for about 4 minutes or until the bottom of the omelet sets. Flip over and fry for a minute or two on the other side. Serve warm.

Eija Patties To the same egg and herb batter, add one potato, grated and squeezed thoroughly or cooked and mashed. This will thicken the batter for making small patties. Fry 2-3 patties at a time, remove from the pan and drain on paper towel.

Shawarma Style Wrap

Chef Guy Perez, Culinary Consultant

Making authentic shawarma requires a special piece of equipment: a huge slowly rotating vertical skewer that is heated on all sides. This version can be made easily at home, and tortillas can substitute for the traditional pita.

Ingredients (serves 4)
450 g (1 lb) top quality beef, such as aged entrecote or sirloin, cut into thin strips
4 onions, slice thinly
Oil
1/4 cup parsley, chopped
4 wheat tortillas
3 tablespoons green tahini dip (p. 9)
2 tomatoes, sliced
1/4 teaspoon cinnamon
1/4 teaspoon ground cumin
1/4 teaspoon curry powder
Salt and freshly ground black pepper

1. Thoroughly heat a heavy iron skillet or griddle and brush lightly with oil.
2. Fry the onions until golden, add the meat and the spices and stir-fry for 3 minutes. Add the parsley, mix well and remove from the skillet. Keep warm.
3. Heat the tortillas on the same skillet, one minute on each side, until they become flexible.
4. Spread each tortilla with one tablespoon of green tahini dip, pile on one-quarter of the meat and onion mixture and arrange a few slices of tomatoes on top of the meat. Wrap tightly in a piece of parchment paper, twist both ends like a candy wrapper, cut the wrap diagonally and serve at once.

Schnitzel

In Israel, schnitzel, and basically anything that's breaded and pan-fried, is right there at the top alongside hummus and other favorite dishes. Real Viennese schnitzel is made from thin slices of veal tenderloin. In Israel it's made from chicken or turkey breast — an invention born out of necessity when veal was nonexistent and poultry was government-subsidized and more readily available. Chicken schnitzel is still the most popular lunch among children and adults alike. Try these recipes and you'll see why. A great many dishes can be made ahead. Not this one. Reheated schnitzel loses all its charm.

Ingredients (serves 4)
2 chicken breasts, halved and pounded flat
2 eggs
Salt and freshly ground black pepper
1/2 cup flour
1 cup breadcrumbs (preferably fresh)
Oil for semi-deep-frying

1. Beat the eggs in a bowl with 2 tablespoons water and season with salt and pepper.
2. Put the flour and breadcrumbs in separate dishes. Dip the pieces of chicken in the flour, shake off the excess, dip in the beaten egg, and finally dip in the breadcrumbs and press firmly to ensure good adhesion of a uniform coating.
3. Pour oil into a heavy frying pan to half the height of the schnitzels. Heat to a medium-high temperature.
4. Fry the schnitzels for 2-3 minutes on each side until golden. Remove from the pan and place on paper towel to drain off the excess oil. Serve promptly with lemon wedges.

To prepare fresh breadcrumbs remove the crusts from a couple of slices of white bread (challah is the best) and crush them in a food processor for half a minute.

Variations
Add 1 teaspoon of Dijon mustard to the beaten eggs
Add 1-2 tablespoons of grated lemon rind to the breadcrumbs
Add 1-2 tablespoons of sesame seeds to the breadcrumbs
Marinate chicken for 2-3 hours in a mixture of olive oil, crushed garlic, lemon juice and fresh herbs (basil, thyme, oregano, etc.)

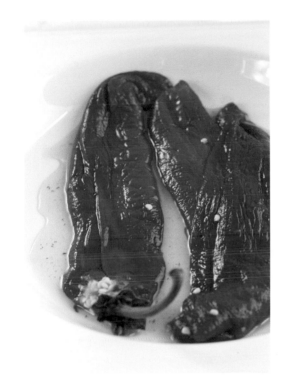

Stuffed Pepper Schnitzel

Also known as "fake schnitzel", this version is golden and crispy on the outside, red and juicy on the inside.

Ingredients (serves 8)

10 sweet red peppers (elongated Shushka peppers are the best, but bell peppers can be used as well)
Olive oil for frying

The Filling:
225 g (8 oz) cream cheese
250 g (9 oz) cottage cheese
200 g (7 oz) hard cheese (gauda or similar), grated
Freshly ground black pepper

The Breading:
2 cups breadcrumbs (preferably fresh)
4 tablespoons sesame seeds
Salt and freshly ground black pepper
2-3 eggs, beaten
Oil for frying

1. Roast the peppers over an open flame or under the oven broiler until the skins blister and peel off. Allow to cool in a plastic bag or a covered bowl. Peel the skins and remove the seeds and membranes. Try to keep the peppers whole, but if they break don't worry — the breading will glue everything back together. Chill well.
2. Mix the filling ingredients thoroughly and season with pepper.
3. Pat the peppers dry with a paper towel. Make a cut the length of each pepper, stuff it with the cheese filling and close the pepper.
4. Prepare separate dishes of the beaten eggs and the breadcrumbs mixed with sesame seeds and seasoned with salt and pepper.
5. Dip the peppers in the breadcrumbs, then in the beaten egg, and then again in the breadcrumbs. Press firmly between your hands to ensure good adhesion of a uniform coating.
6. Pour oil into a heavy frying pan to half the height of the schnitzels. Heat to medium temperature.
7. Fry the pepper schnitzels 2-3 minutes on each side, until golden. Remove from the oil, drain the excess on paper towel and serve promptly.

Variation Stuff the peppers with sliced mozzarella or soft fresh goat cheese.

Chicken Laffa Wrap with Spinach and Pine Nuts

In this typical Middle Eastern wrap, the chicken filling is seasoned with cumin, coriander and garlic. Tortillas are a nice alternative to Iraqi laffa bread.

Ingredients (serves 4)
350 grams (12 oz) ground chicken (preferably deboned thighs)
3 tablespoons olive oil
2 large onions, chopped coarsely
2 cloves garlic, chopped
1/3 cup pine nuts, roasted
1/4 cup dried cranberries
1 hot pepper, chopped
1 tablespoon dry coriander seeds, ground
1 tablespoon dry cumin seeds, ground
Salt and freshly ground black pepper
500 g (1 lb) fresh spinach leaves, washed and chopped
1/4 cup fresh basil leaves, cut into strips
To Serve:
2 pieces laffa (Iraqi pita bread), each cut into two, or 4 wheat tortillas
Tahini dip (p. 9)

1. Heat the olive oil in a large frying pan or wok and stir-fry the chicken, continuously breaking it down with a fork.
2. Add the onions and fry for about 10 minutes. Add the garlic, pine nuts and cranberries, season with the hot pepper, ground coriander, cumin, salt and pepper. Add the spinach and basil, toss for 2 minutes and remove from the stove.
3. Fill each laffa half or tortilla with one-quarter of the filling and roll into a wrap. Serve with tahini.

FAMILY DINNERS

Chicken and Vegetable Soup with Egg Droplets

A rich, colorful soup with a touch of Yemenite spice that adds a surprisingly piquant flavor to the egg droplets.

Ingredients (serves 6-8)

3 tablespoons oil
1 leek (white part only), sliced
4 carrots, diced
4 zucchini, sliced
500 g (1 lb) pumpkin, cut into large cubes
5 celery stalks (with some of the leaves), sliced
1/2 cup parsley, chopped
1 parsley root, cut coarsely
1 heaping tablespoon hawaij spice mix for soup (see opposite)
21/2 liters (21/2 quarts) chicken soup

The Egg Droplets:

2-3 eggs
Salt and coarsely ground black pepper
1/4 teaspoon hawaij spice mix for soup
1/2 cup flour

1. Heat the oil in a large saucepan. Add the vegetables and sauté briefly, until the edges start to brown. Add the hawaij and sauté for about 5 minutes.
2. Pour in the soup, bring to a boil and lower the heat. Skim the fat and foam that form on the top, and cook, partly covered, for about 30 minutes.
3. **Prepare the egg droplets:** In a bowl, mix the eggs, salt, pepper and hawaij. Add the flour gradually while stirring, to form a thick batter.
4. Bring the soup to a steady boil and, using two oiled teaspoons, quickly form egg droplets and slide into the soup. Cook for 10-12 minutes, until the egg droplets float on top. Serve hot.

Hawaij Spice Mix for Soup

1 tablespoon ground black pepper
1 tablespoon ground cumin
1/2 tablespoon ground cardamom
1/2 tablespoon ground caraway
3/4 tablespoon ground turmeric
1/2 tablespoon ground coriander seeds
1/2 teaspoon ground cloves
1/2 tablespoon ground dried coriander leaves

Mix all the ingredients and keep in an airtight jar.

Vegetable Soup with Kubbe Dumplings

Your won't need a main course after this comforting wintertime treat. Kubbe (or kibbe) is the collective name for deep-fried or steamed dumplings, found throughout the Middle East. This soft semolina kubbe comes from the Kurdish kitchen. Making the dumplings takes time and effort, so prepare a double amount (like in this recipe) and freeze what's left.

Ingredients (serves 8-10)
The Kubbe Dough:

31/2 cups semolina
100 g (31/2 oz) butter, softened
1/2 cup oil
Salt and freshly ground black pepper
1 tablespoon chicken soup mix (optional)
3/4 cup lukewarm water

The Filling:

3 tablespoons oil
2 onions, chopped very finely
500 g (1 lb) beef, ground finely
Salt and freshly ground black pepper
1/2 cup fresh coriander, chopped

The Soup:

500 g (1 lb) pumpkin, peeled and cut in chunks
3 zucchini, sliced
1 bunch of celery stalks, with the leaves, sliced 2 cm (1 inch) thick
3 tablespoons oil
1 large onion, diced
5 ripe tomatoes, peeled and diced
1 tablespoon chicken soup mix
1 tablespoon onion soup mix
1 cup fresh coriander, chopped

1. **Prepare the dough:** Mix all the ingredients and knead well into soft pliable dough. If the dough is too dry, add some water. Set aside.

2. **Prepare the filling:** Heat the oil in a skillet and brown the onion for 5 minutes. Add the meat and sauté for a few minutes, using a fork to break it down into crumbs. Remove from the stove and season with salt, pepper and chopped coriander. Set aside.

3. **Prepare the soup:** In a large soup pot, boil the pumpkin, zucchini and celery in 21/2 liters of water.

4. Meanwhile, fry the onion in a separate pan until translucent, add the tomatoes and cook over a low flame until the sauce is red and thick. Transfer the sauce to the soup pot, add the chicken soup mix and the onion soup mix and cook for 20 minutes on medium heat, with the pot partly covered.

5. **Prepare the kubbe:** Dip your hands in cold water. Put a piece of dough the size of a large egg in the palm of your left hand and press your right thumb into its center to create a hole for the filling. Put a tablespoon of filling in the hole and reshape the dough into a ball.

6. Slide half the quantity of dumplings into the boiling soup and simmer until they float on the surface (remember, you doubled the dough recipe for future use). Lower the heat and cook for 15 minutes. Turn off the heat, add the coriander, and wait 5 minutes before serving.

Ptitim Salad with Herbs

Israelis find it amazing that the humble ptitim, known outside the country as Israeli couscous, was for a time a sought-after gourmet ingredient in posh restaurants in New York and London. Literally "small flakes" in Hebrew, these toasted pasta flakes were invented in Israel shortly after the War of Independence when they substituted for rice in the period of economic hardship. Today, decades later, they are still popular. Usually served hot, ptitim also make a base for a filling salad. This one is lovely — lemony and fragrant with an abundance of fresh herbs.

Ingredients (serves 6)

2 cups ptitim (Israeli couscous)
3 carrots cut into juliennes
3 spring onions, sliced thinly
1 cup black Greek olives
1/2 cup fresh coriander, chopped
1/2 cup fresh parsley, chopped
6 sprigs basil, chopped
1/2 cup olive oil
3 tablespoons sesame oil
3 tablespoons nigella and sesame seeds, toasted
Juice and zest from 2 lemons
Salt and freshly ground black pepper

1. Cook the ptitim in a large quantity of salted boiling water (like you would pasta) until tender. Rinse under running water until cool and drain.
2. Transfer to a bowl and pour on a little oil to prevent the ptitim from sticking. Add the rest of the ingredients and toss well. Adjust seasoning and set aside for at least half an hour before serving.

Mejadra —
Rice with Lentils

This Middle Eastern specialty is usually served as a side dish, but can be a highly nutritious main course for vegetarians, or for all of us for that matter.

Ingredients (serves 6-8)
1 cup brown lentils
2 cups rice
Olive oil for frying
3 onions, chopped
1 tablespoon ground cumin
Salt and freshly ground black pepper
To Serve (optional):
2 onions, thinly sliced
Oil for frying

1. Cook the lentils in water until they soften, about 30 minutes. Drain and set aside.
2. Heat the olive oil in a saucepan and fry the onions until golden. Add the lentils and season with cumin, salt and pepper. Add the rice and stir-fry for a minute or two until the rice grains turn opaque.
3. Add 3 cups boiling water, bring to a boil, lower the heat, cover and cook for 20 minutes. Turn off the heat, fluff with a fork, cover and let rest for 10 minutes before serving.
4. Before serving, fry the onion rings in oil until brown and crisp and arrange over the mejadra.

Quick Mejadra If you have cooked rice on hand, use it to prepare mejadra. Cook lentils until they soften. Fry the onions, add the lentils and season. Add the rice and heat together for about 5 minutes.

Stuffed Zucchini in Sweet and Sour Apricot Sauce

A rich stuffing of chicken, rice and herbs and a tangy fruit sauce create a dish that is both attractive and delicious. Round zucchini are very convenient for stuffing, but if unavailable regular ones will do. Follow step by step photos on page 74.

Ingredients (makes 12 portions)
12 medium round zucchini
The Stuffing:
500 g (1 lb) chicken, ground coarsely
1 large onion, grated
1/3 cup coriander, chopped finely
1/3 cup fresh parsley, chopped finely
3/4 cup rice
1 pinch lemon salt
1 teaspoon Hawaij spice mix for soup
(Yemenite spice mix, p. 65)
Salt and crushed black pepper
The Sauce:
3 tablespoons oil
1 large onion, chopped finely
3 cloves garlic
1 cup dried apricots, chopped finely
6 fresh ripe tomatoes, grated coarsely
The juice and zest of 1 large lemon
1 heaping tablespoon sugar
1 teaspoon Hawaij spice mix for soup (p. 65)
Salt and crushed black pepper
2-3 cups clear chicken soup or stock

1. Cut off the tops of the zucchini to form lids. Core the zucchini using a teaspoon or melon baller, leaving 1/2 cm (1/4 inch) thick walls. Save the cored flesh for the sauce. Save the lids.
2. Mix all the stuffing ingredients and stuff the zucchini loosely; the rice will swell during cooking.
3. **Prepare the sauce:** Heat the oil in a wide shallow saucepan and fry the onions until golden. Add the garlic and chopped apricots and fry for one minute. Add the tomatoes, lemon, sugar and spices and bring to a boil.
4. Spread the flesh scooped out of the zucchini over the sauce. Arrange the stuffed zucchini in a single layer over the flesh. Put the "lids" next to the zucchini. Pour the soup into the pan. Place a plate directly over the zucchini and cover the pan. Bring to a boil, lower the flame and cook for about 45 minutes until the rice is very tender. Put the lids on and serve hot.

Chicken Patties with Swiss Chard, Leeks and Celery

Made from beef or chicken, fried, grilled or steamed, served on a bed of rice or couscous, or even (you guessed it!) stuffed in a pita, patties are the very epitome of local home cooking. In this summertime recipe, chicken patties are cooked in a fragrant, slightly sour broth brimming with leafy greens.

Ingredients (serves 6-8)

The Sauce:
3 tablespoons oil
2 leeks (white part only), cut into large chunks
1 bunch celery (stalks and leaves), cut coarsely
1 bunch Swiss chard (stalks and leaves), cut coarsely
2 tablespoons sugar
1/2 cup freshly squeezed lemon juice
2 cups clear chicken soup or stock
Salt and freshly ground black pepper

The Patties:
500 g (1 lb) ground chicken
1 egg yolk
2 tablespoons breadcrumbs
Salt and white pepper
1 teaspoon dry coriander seeds, ground

1. **Prepare the sauce:** Heat the oil in a large wide saucepan and sauté the leeks for 5 minutes, stirring frequently. Add the celery and Swiss chard and continue sautéing for 5 more minutes. Add sugar, lemon juice and chicken soup, season with salt and pepper, and cook on low heat until the vegetables are tender, about 15 minutes.

2. **Prepare the patties:** While the sauce is cooking, mix the ingredients for the patties and knead well.

3. Form small patties, slide into the sauce, cover and cook over low heat for about 30 minutes. Turn off the heat and wait 10 minutes before serving.

Variation Fry the patties briefly in a small amount of oil, only until they turn golden, before adding them to the sauce.

Stuffed Zucchini in Sweet and Sour
Apricot Sauce (p. 72)

Grilled Fish Stuffed with Pickled Lemons

Meggi Bibi, Meggi & Tuly Catering

Family cookouts (*mangal*) are our favorite pastime, especially on sunny weekends. Shish kebabs, chicken wings, lamb kebabs and steaks are the meats of choice on these occasions, but grilled fish is becoming increasingly popular. In this recipe gilthead sea bream (locally called *denis*) is used because it is readily available in Israel, but any other white-fleshed fish will work equally well.

Ingredients (serves 4)

4 whole gilthead sea breams or other portion-size firm-fleshed saltwater fish, gutted and cleaned thoroughly
Salt and freshly ground black pepper
Fresh herbs: sprigs of thyme, rosemary and parsley
1/2 cup pickled lemons (p. 49)
Olive oil for brushing

1. Season the cavity of each fish with salt and pepper and stuff with pickled lemon slices and herbs.
2. Make 2-3 diagonal slits on each side of the fish and rub with oil mixed with salt and pepper.
3. Heat charcoal grill, brush with oil, and barbeque the fish for 6 minutes on each side. It is advisable to drip some olive oil on the fish during grilling. Serve at once.

Variation Purée some pickled lemons and serve as a dipping sauce with the fish.

Chreime — North African Hot Fish Stew

Juicy fish chunks cooked in a fiery red and very spicy sauce. Chreime made from grouper, amberjack or some other fine fish is featured at Rosh Hashanah and Passover dinners in the households of North African Jews (from Morocco, Libya, Algeria, Tunisia), but the sauce is so delicious and dominant that inexpensive fish may be used. The cooking time must be adapted to the type of fish: the leaner the fish, the shorter the cooking cycle.

The dominant spices in chreime are paprika, cayenne pepper and garlic, but the secret ingredient that never fails to give the sauce the touch of authenticity is ground caraway.

Ingredients (serves 4-6)
1 kg (2 lb 4 oz) fish with white, firm flesh (grouper, greater amberjack, sea bass, grey mullet or even carp), cut through the bone into thick slices (steaks)
1/3 cup oil
10 cloves garlic, crushed
2 tablespoons paprika
1 tablespoon (or less) cayenne pepper
1 teaspoon ground caraway
1 teaspoon ground cumin (optional)
2-3 tablespoons tomato paste

1. Heat the oil in a large wide saucepan, add the garlic and spices and fry over high heat while stirring until the oil becomes aromatic. Add the tomato paste and stir until the paste blends with the oil. Add one cup of water and cook covered for 5 minutes.
2. Carefully add the fish steaks to the sauce, bring to a boil, cover and lower the heat. If the sauce does not completely cover the fish steaks, turn them once halfway through the cooking.
3. Cook for 10 minutes or until the fish is done but still firm and juicy. Serve with couscous or steamed rice and a lot of soft white bread for mopping up the sauce.

Making the Best of Instant Couscous

Thank goodness for instant couscous. It has made this North African staple accessible to everyone, not just households graced with experienced Moroccan or Tunisian cooks. Here's a method that will make it even better: Measure out the couscous and combine it with an equal amount of boiling water. Season with salt and a few saffron threads and mix well. Set aside for 10 minutes, add oil (3 tablespoons for 500 g/1 lb couscous) and mix again. Rub the couscous between your palms to make smaller uniform crumbs and fluff with a fork. Cook in a couscoussier (a double boiler fitted with a sieve) over boiling water or aromatic stock or heat covered in a microwave. Fluff again before serving.

Couscous Salad with Chickpeas, Raisins and Feta Cheese

Appetizing and satisfying, this salad can be made ahead and kept in the fridge.

Ingredients (serves 6)
1 small packet (350 g, 12 oz) instant couscous, medium grain
1 cup chickpeas soaked in water overnight
1 cup raisins
2 tablespoon dry coriander seeds
Zest from 1 lemon
1/4 cup fresh coriander leaves, chopped
The Dressing:
1/4 cup olive oil
1/3 cup freshly squeezed lemon juice
2 teaspoons ground cumin
Salt and freshly ground black pepper
To Serve:
250 g (9 oz) brinza or feta cheese

1. Cook the chickpeas in a large quantity of water until tender (about 2 hours).
2. Prepare the couscous according to the manufacturers' instructions but do not season. Transfer to a large bowl and fluff with a fork.
3. Add chickpeas, raisins, coriander seeds, lemon zest and chopped coriander.
4. Mix the ingredients for the dressing and pour over the salad. Toss well and adjust seasoning. Sprinkle with the cheese before serving.

Couscous with Mafroum

Mafroum are potatoes or eggplants stuffed with ground meat and cooked in a spicy red sauce. This gem hails from Tunisian/Libyan Jewish cuisine and is traditionally served over a bed of couscous that absorbs the delicious liquids.

Ingredients (serves 6)
500 g (1 lb) instant couscous
The Potatoes:
6 medium potatoes (of uniform size)
Salt and freshly ground black pepper
Flour
2 eggs, beaten
Oil for semi-deep-frying
The Stuffing:
500 g (1 lb) lean beef, finely ground
1 cup fresh parsley, chopped
Salt and freshly ground black pepper to taste
2/3 teaspoon Baharat seasoning mix (see opposite page)

1/3 teaspoon ground turmeric
1 potato, grated and drained thoroughly
The Sauce:
1 large onion, chopped
4 cloves garlic, crushed
4 stalks celery, peeled and cut coarsely
3 tablespoons tomato paste
1/2 cup tomatoes, diced
1/2 tablespoon sweet paprika
Salt
1/2 teaspoon ground cinnamon
Dry chili pepper to taste
1/2 teaspoon ground ginger
One-quarter of a cabbage, cut coarsely
1-11/2 liters (1-11/2 quarts) chicken stock or water
3 tablespoons fresh mint, chopped
3 tablespoons fresh parsley, chopped
3 tablespoons fresh celery leaves, coarsely chopped

1. **Prepare the mafroum potatoes:** Mix all the stuffing ingredients and knead thoroughly. Set aside for at least half an hour to blend the flavors.

2. Cut the potatoes lengthwise. Slit each half almost all the way to create two halves connected at one end.

3. Stuff the potatoes with the meat mixture so the open side of the "sandwich" becomes thicker (see photograph)

4. Heat oil for semi-deep-frying in a wide saucepan.

5. Dip in flour and then in beaten egg. Fry until golden-brown, turning once. Remove from the pan and drain the excess oil on paper towel.

6. **Prepare the sauce:** Pour out most of the frying oil. Sauté the onion in the remaining oil until translucent. Add the garlic and celery stalks and fry for 4 minutes. Add the tomato paste and diced tomato, stir, lower the heat, cover and cook for 10 minutes.

7. Season and add the cabbage and chicken stock (or water). Cook partly covered for 20 minutes. Add the mint, parsley and celery leaves.

8. Arrange the potatoes in a single layer in the saucepan and bring to a boil. Cover and cook for two hours over low heat until the potatoes are tender.

9. **To serve:** Prepare the couscous according to the manufacturer's instructions. Set out the mafroum potatoes, the sauce and the couscous in separate serving dishes. Let each guest take some couscous and top it with the mafroum potatoes and sauce.

Mafroum Eggplants Slice two eggplants into 2-3 cm (1 1/2 inch) thick slices. Cut each slice across, but not all the way, to form a sandwich bun (see the instructions for mafroum potatoes). Continue according to the recipe for mafroum potatoes, but shorten the cooking time to one hour to keep the eggplant slices from falling apart.

Baharat Spice Mix

It is best to use whole spices and roast and grind them prior to mixing, but quality ground spices can be used as well.

1 tablespoon ground cardamom
1 tablespoon ground black pepper
1/2 tablespoon ground allspice
1 tablespoon ground cinnamon
1 tablespoon ground dry ginger
1/2 tablespoon ground nutmeg

Mix all the ingredients and store in an airtight jar.

Chicken and Olives Tagine

Chef Guy Peretz, Culinary Consultant

Inspired by a famous Moroccan dish, this piquant chicken casserole is impressive yet easy to make. If you don't have a traditional clay tagine, use an ordinary casserole dish.

Ingredients (serves 4-6)
1 chicken, cut into 8 parts
1 cup green olives (preferably the bitter Souri variety), cracked and pitted
1/2 teaspoon turmeric
4 tablespoons olive oil
6 cloves garlic, sliced
1/2 chili pepper, chopped
1 lemon, peeled, seeded and chopped
1/4 teaspoon salt
1/4 teaspoon white pepper
2 bay leaves
4 tablespoons fresh coriander

1. Preheat oven to 180°C (350°F).
2. Blanch the olives in boiling water with 1/4 teaspoon turmeric for 2-3 minutes. Drain and set aside.
3. Heat the oil in a large deep skillet and brown the chicken parts on all sides. Add the garlic and chili pepper and fry until golden. Add lemon, salt, pepper, bay leaves and the remaining turmeric, mix well and sauté until fragrant.
4. Add one cup of water to the skillet and bring to a boil. Transfer the contents of the pan to a tagine or an ovenproof casserole with a close-fitting lid. Bake for 40 minutes, until the chicken is done. Serve on a bed of couscous or rice.

Kugel with Honey and Raisins

A homey yet lush rendition of a traditional Jewish noodle casserole. Freshly ground black pepper (hallmark of the Jerusalem kugel) enhances the sweetness of raisins and honey.

Ingredients (for a square 20 cm/8 inch pan or 2 loaf pans)
400 g (1 lb) flat noodles
1/2 cup oil
1/2 cup honey
1/2 cup light brown sugar
4 eggs, beaten
1-2 teaspoons freshly ground black pepper
1 cup dark raisins

1. Preheat oven to 170°C (325°F).
2. Cook the noodles in a large quantity of boiling water until tender but still firm (al dente). Rinse, drain and transfer to a bowl.
3. In a small pot, bring oil, honey and sugar to a simmer, stirring constantly, and continue cooking until the sugar melts and the mixture is caramel colored. Pour over the noodles and mix well.
4. Add the eggs, raisins and pepper and transfer to a greased baking dish.
5. Cover with foil and bake for half an hour, until the top is golden and crispy. Serve promptly, or store covered with foil and heat for 10 minutes in a medium-hot oven just before serving.

THE FESTIVE TABLE

Homage to Chopped Liver

The inspiration is clearly *gehakte leber* — the much loved Jewish delicacy — but instead of chopping the ingredients, they are layered to create a light and attractive starter fit for an elegant dinner.

Ingredients (serves 8-10)
250 g (9 oz) frozen puff pastry, thawed
1 large egg, lightly beaten with a tablespoon of water and a dash of salt
500 g (1 lb) chicken livers, separated into lobes, trimmed, and rinsed
1/2 cup oil
5 large onions, chopped
1-2 tablespoons sweet red wine or port
Salt and freshly ground black pepper
2 eggs (preferably free range, with bright yellow yolks)
Spring onions, sliced, for garnish

1. Heat 1/2 cup oil in a heavy skillet. Add onions and sauté on medium heat for 15 minutes until golden. Be careful not to scorch the onions or they will get bitter.
2. Add the livers and sauté until they are done, about 5 minutes. Add the wine and season with salt and pepper. Remove from the stove and let cool.
3. Meanwhile, boil the eggs in salted water for 7-8 minutes. Don't overcook them or the yolks will turn greenish. Cool in a bowl of water.
4. Preheat oven to 180°C (350°F).
5. Roll out the pastry, and using a cookie cutter or a glass, make a dozen 8 cm (3 inch) disks.
6. Brush with egg and bake for 10-15 minutes until golden and puffy.
7. Peel and slice the eggs.
8. **To serve:** Layer each warm pastry disc with a slice of egg and one liver lobe and some of the fried onion. Garnish with spring onion and serve while the pastry is still warm.

Figs, Wild Rice and Roquefort Salad in Silan Vinaigrette

Figs and Roquefort cheese make a great couple. In this salad they are joined by wild rice, toasted almonds and crunchy celery, and dressed in honeyed vinaigrette. What a feast!

Ingredients (serves 4-6)
12 ripe figs, quartered lengthwise or sliced
3 stalks celery, diced
1 cup cooked wild rice, chilled
1 cup sunflower sprouts (optional)
1/4 cup sliced almonds, lightly toasted
50 g (2 oz) Roquefort cheese, crumbled

The Vinaigrette:
6 tablespoons delicate olive oil
2 tablespoons white wine vinegar
3 tablespoon silan (see below) or 21/2 tablespoons honey
1 clove garlic, chopped
Salt and freshly ground black pepper

1. Arrange the figs on a large semi-deep serving plate and sprinkle the rest of the ingredients on top.
2. Whisk the vinaigrette ingredients until smooth and drizzle over the salad. Serve at once.

Silan (Date Honey) A very thick sweet syrup made from dried dates, similar to honey but darker in color and with a pronounced caramel taste. It is used as a color and flavor enhancer in slow-cooking dishes like hamin, or in any recipe calling for honey, caramel, molasses or syrup. If unavailable, it can be substituted by honey. Historians believe that the "honey" in the "Land of Milk and Honey" is actually silan.

Eggplant Soup with Feta, Mint and Sumac

Velvety, smooth , and with a delicate smoky touch, this truly delectable soup features some of the trendiest ingredients of the new Israeli cuisine. Serve it hot or at room temperature.

Ingredients (serves 6)
4 eggplants
50 g (2 oz) butter
1 onion, coarsely chopped
2 cloves garlic, sliced
1 cup strong tasting yogurt (preferably sheep or goat milk)
Salt and freshly ground black pepper
To serve:
250 g (9 oz) feta cheese, crumbled
2-3 tablespoons mint leaves
Dash of sumac

1. Wrap each eggplant in aluminum foil and roast on an open fire until soft (turn once or twice to make sure they roast evenly). Cool and scoop out the flesh. Drain in a colander for 30 minutes to get rid of the liquid.
2. Melt the butter in a pan on low heat. Add onion and garlic and sauté gently for 10 minutes, stirring frequently, until they turn translucent.
3. Pour in 31/2 cups of water, add the eggplants and bring to a boil. Cover, reduce the heat to minimum and simmer for 20 minutes.
4. Add the yogurt and purée the soup in a food processor until smooth. Season with salt and pepper and refrigerate.
5. **To serve:** Warm gently: do not bring to a full boil. Taste and adjust seasoning. Pour into serving bowls, sprinkle with feta cheese, mint leaves and sumac. To serve at room temperature, remove from the refrigerator one hour before eating.

Tzaziki with Grapes and Almonds

Shmil Holland, "Shmil in the Lab", Jerusalem

Tzaziki is a chilled yogurt soup served throughout the Balkans and very common in Israel. This version, prepared with frozen grapes and crunchy almonds, is fit for a special occasion. Flavorful thick yogurt is the key to success. Three different kinds are combined here — cow's milk, goat or sheep and buffalo — but you can substitute other kinds according to personal taste and availability.

Ingredients (serves 6-8)

2 cups cow's milk yogurt
2 cups goat or sheep milk yogurt
2 cups buffalo milk yogurt
1/3 cup olive oil
Sea salt
Freshly squeezed lemon juice to taste
Grated zest of half a lemon
3 sprigs mint, chopped
3 sprigs dill, chopped
3 cloves garlic, crushed
1 cup green grapes without stems, frozen
300 g (11 oz) cucumbers, peeled and diced finely
1/2 cup chives, chopped
3 tablespoons blanched slivered almonds, chopped

1. Combine 3 kinds of yogurt. Gradually whisk in the olive oil (similar to making mayonnaise) until smooth. The oil must be completely blended or it will float on the surface.
2. Season with salt and stir in the lemon juice and zest, mint, dill and garlic. Up to this point the soup can be kept refrigerated for as long as 24 hours.
3. When ready to serve, halve the frozen grapes and put them together with the diced cucumbers into serving bowls, saving some of the grapes for garnish. Pour the yogurt on top and garnish with chives, chopped almonds and the remaining grapes.

Fish Kebabs on a Bed of Bulgur and Black Lentils

Daniela Nir Paz, Catering Gratzia

Fish kebabs served with yogurt or tahini sauce have become all the rage in local restaurants. This version is a bit off the beaten track: the fish patties are served on a cinnamon stick, which adds aroma and turns the kebabs into a perfect snack for cocktails and picnics. The yogurt sauce is bright violet thanks to the beetroot, and the bulgur and black lentils side dish is so nice you might want to serve it with other mains.

Ingredients (serves 6)

The Kebabs:

500 g (1 lb) fillet of white-fleshed saltwater fish (red snapper, grouper, sea bream)
1 large onion, chopped
1 clove garlic, chopped
4 tablespoons polenta
1 cup chopped herbs: mint, coriander, parsley
Salt and freshly ground black pepper
6 long cinnamon sticks

Bulgur with Lentils:

1/2 cup black lentils soaked overnight in water and drained
1 cup bulgur wheat, soaked for 1/2 hour in water and drained
2 tablespoons olive oil
1 onion, chopped
1 clove garlic, crushed
1/2 teaspoon baharat spice mix (p. 83)
Salt and freshly ground black pepper

The Yogurt and Beetroot Sauce:

1 beetroot, cooked and peeled
1 cup thick yogurt
Salt and freshly ground black pepper

1. **Prepare the kebabs:** Grind the fish in a meat grinder. If you use a food processor, work in short pulses to retain a slightly chunky texture. Add the rest of the ingredients and mix well. Wet your hands and make six oval patties. Insert a cinnamon stick into each one. Refrigerate until ready to use.

2. **Prepare the bulgur:** Cook the lentils in slightly salted boiling water for 10 minutes, until just tender. Drain and set aside.

3. Heat the oil in a skillet and sauté the onions and garlic until translucent. Add the lentils and the bulgur, season with baharat, salt and pepper, and heat through, stirring constantly. Remove from the stove and cover.

4. **Prepare the dressing:** Purée the beetroot with the yogurt and season with salt and pepper.

5. **To serve:** Brush the kebabs with oil and barbeque on a hot charcoal grill, under the oven broiler, or on a very hot cast iron skillet for 4-5 minutes, turning once or twice until ready. Serve with warm bulgur and lentils and garnish with the yogurt sauce.

Creamy Jerusalem Artichoke Soup

Chef Avi Steinitz

Golden, smooth and creamy, this soup can also be served in espresso cups as an appetizer.

Ingredients (for 10 espresso cups or 4-6 soup bowls)
750 g (11/2 lb) Jerusalem artichokes, peeled and cut into 4 cm (2 inch) pieces
2 tablespoons olive oil
2 cloves garlic, peeled
1 leek (white part only), finely chopped
2 cups vegetable stock
1/2 cup whipping cream
Salt and white pepper
The Garnish (Jerusalem artichoke chips):
2 Jerusalem artichokes, peeled and shaved with a vegetable peeler
Oil for deep-frying

1. Heat oil in a heavy saucepan and sauté the chopped leeks until translucent. Add the garlic and sauté for one more minute. Add the Jerusalem artichokes and sauté for a few more minutes.
2. Add the stock and bring to a boil. Season with a little salt and pepper, cover, and cook for 30 minutes over low heat until the artichokes are very tender.
3. Purée the soup in a food processor and strain. Bring to a boil, add the cream, taste and adjust the seasoning.
4. **Prepare the garnish:** Heat the oil for deep-frying and fry the artichoke shavings until crisp. Drain excess oil on paper towel.

Jerusalem artichoke has nothing to do with Jerusalem, or with artichokes for that matter. Originally from North America, this tasty tuber is in fact a member of the sunflower family. Girasole, Italian for sunflower, sounds like Jerusalem, hence the mix-up. In Israel it has gained popularity over the last few decades, mainly in restaurants, usually as a soup or a purée.

Grilled Chicken Thighs with Apricot and Lemon Grass Sauce

Chef Segev Moshe, Segev Restaurant, Herzliya, Segev Express Tel Aviv

Nicknamed by local cooks *pargiyot* (literally spring chickens), deboned chicken thighs, with their dark juicy meat and relatively high fat content, are ideal for grilling, broiling and barbequing. Talented Segev Moshe paired them with fresh apricots poached in a fragrant mixture of lemon grass and orange juice.

Ingredients (serves 4)
4 deboned chicken thighs, 200 g (7 oz) each
Oil for brushing
Salt and freshly ground black pepper
The Sauce:
2 tablespoons olive oil
3 tablespoons chopped lemon grass (use only the bottom part of peeled stalks)
1/3 cup pine nuts
2 cups freshly squeezed orange juice
2 cloves garlic, sliced
2 sprigs thyme
8 whole apricots
Baby greens for garnish

1. **Prepare the sauce:** Heat olive oil in a large skillet over high heat. Sauteé the lemon grass for 1 minute, until fragrant. Add pine nuts and stir-fry until golden. Add the orange juice, garlic and thyme, lower the heat and simmer for 2-3 minutes until the sauce thickens slightly.
2. Add the apricots and cook until they are glazed in the sauce, about 5 minutes.
3. While the apricots are cooking, flatten the chicken pieces slightly, brush with oil on both sides, season with salt and pepper, and fry in a hot cast iron skillet or under a hot broiler until done. Turn once.
4. **To serve:** Put a chicken steak on a warmed plate, pour the sauce on top and add 2 apricots. Garnish with baby greens and serve at once. Warn your guests that the apricots are not pitted.

Variation If apricots are not in season, use 4 halved, pitted peaches. Slightly tangy, yellow fleshed varieties are the most suitable.

Lamb Neck and Root Vegetables Casserole

Chef Avi Steinitz

Succulent chunks of lamb and fragrant root vegetables glazed in a rich sauce come together to create a casserole fit for a king.

Ingredients (serves 8)

11/2 kg (3 lb) lamb neck cut into 16 slices
Olive oil or goose fat, for frying
Flour, for dredging
Salt and freshly ground black pepper
2 onions, chopped
1 tablespoon tomato purée
3 cups dry red wine
1 liter (1 quart) lamb or beef stock
1 celery root, cut into large dice
6 parsley roots, halved lengthwise
12 small carrots, peeled
8 shallots, peeled
3-4 tomatoes, peeled and chopped, seeds and juice removed
5 sprigs thyme
3 garlic heads, cut across the middle
4 bay leaves

1. Heat the olive oil in a large heavy casserole. Dredge the lamb in flour seasoned with salt and pepper. Shake off the excess flour and brown 2-3 minutes on each side. Set aside.
2. In the same saucepan, brown the onions, add the tomato purée and fry, stirring occasionally. Pour in the wine and scrape the bottom of the saucepan to deglaze the sauce. Continue cooking until the liquids have reduced slightly. Add the meat, pour in the stock, cover and cook over a low flame for an hour and a half.
3. In a frying pan, heat some olive oil and sauté the vegetables with the thyme, garlic and bay leaves until they are glazed, about 5-10 minutes. Season with salt and pepper. Add the vegetables to the saucepan with the meat and cook covered for two hours over a low flame, until the meat is very tender and the sauce is thick and shiny.

Leg of Lamb Stuffed with Haroset

Chef Avi Steinitz

Haroset, juicy fruit and nut spoon sweet, is an important part of the Passover ritual. As this recipe shows, it also makes a terrific filling for another symbol on the Seder table — the leg of lamb.

Ingredients (serves 6)
11/2 kg (3 lb) leg of lamb, shank bone left in, hip end of bone removed (have the butcher do this for you)
3 tablespoons olive oil

The Haroset Stuffing:
250 g (9 oz) ground beef or lamb
2 tart baking apples, cored and diced
250 g (9 oz) date paste (see below)
11/4 cups walnuts
Salt and freshly ground black pepper
1/4 teaspoon dry ginger
Leaves from 1 thyme sprig

The Spice Rub:
Salt and freshly ground black pepper
1 sprig rosemary, chopped
1 tablespoon dry coriander seeds
1/2 teaspoon ground chili pepper
2 cloves garlic, crushed
5 tablespoons olive oil

1. Spread the leg of lamb on a work surface (the side with the bone facing up). Mix the stuffing ingredients thoroughly and spread along the center of the leg. Wrap the meat over the stuffing to make an elongated package. Tie with kitchen string.
2. Preheat oven to 180°C (350°F).
3. Combine the spice rub ingredients and rub the meat on all sides.
4. Heat 3 tablespoons olive oil in a large skillet and brown the meat on all sides. Remove from the skillet and wrap loosely in aluminum foil.
5. Roast for 50-60 minutes (a meat thermometer inserted inside the lamb should indicate 60°C/ 140°F for medium). Let rest for 10-15 minutes before carving.

THE FESTIVE TABLE

Herbed Passover Noodles

Chef Avi Steinitz

Easily made at home, these pretty noodles will upgrade a clear chicken soup and also make a nice side dish for meat or fish.

Ingredients (serves 6-8)
4 eggs
4 tablespoons cold water
2 tablespoons thin matzo meal
Salt and freshly ground black pepper
3 heaping spoons chives, thinly chopped
Oil for frying

1. Whisk all ingredients, except the oil, until smooth.
2. Heat a nonstick crêpe pan and brush it with a little oil.
3. Ladle 2-3 spoonfuls of batter into the pan. Tilt and rotate the pan quickly to cover the bottom with a layer of batter and return any excess to the bowl.
4. Return the pan to the heat and cook for 1 minute, or until the top appears almost dry. Turn over and cook the other side lightly. Transfer to a plate. Make crêpes with the remaining batter in the same manner, brushing the pan lightly with oil as necessary. Roll each crêpe in a tight roll and slice thinly. Refrigerate until ready to serve.

To serve Add to boiling chicken soup before serving or toss in a skillet with some olive oil until hot and crispy.

THE FESTIVE TABLE

Eggplant and Cheese Bourekitas

The secret to this exquisite snack is its simplicity: the pastry is delicately crisp and the filling is very lightly seasoned. Don't be tempted to add spices. The flame-roasted eggplants combined with cheese need no enhancement.

Ingredients (makes 50 bourekitas)
The Pastry:
480 ml (17 fl oz, 2 cups) oil
240 ml (81/2 fl oz, 1 cup) water
1/2 teaspoon salt
1 kg (2 lb 4 oz, 7 cups) flour
The Filling:
5 eggplants
80 ml (3 fl oz, 1/3 cup) oil
300 g (101/2 oz) brinza or feta cheese, crumbled
The Coating:
1 egg, beaten
Sesame and nigella seeds

1. **Prepare the pastry:** Pour the oil, water and salt into a large bowl. Gradually add the flour and knead into a soft, nonsticky dough.
2. **Prepare the filling:** Roast the eggplants (see instructions on p. 25), peel and chop them, and drain in a colander for about 30 minutes.
3. Add the oil to the eggplants and mix well. Stir in the cheese.
4. **Prepare the bourekitas:** Preheat the oven to 200°C (400°F).
5. Form about 50 dough balls the size of large apricots and roll them into 12 cm (14 inch) thick disks. Put a spoonful of the filling in the center of each disk, fold into a crescent and pinch the edges to seal.
6. Arrange the bourekitas with sufficient space between them on a tray lined with baking paper. Brush with beaten egg and sprinkle sesame or nigella seeds on top. Bake for 20-25 minutes until golden.

SOMETHING SWEET

Upside-down Apple and Honey Cake

On Rosh Hashana Eve, the Jewish New Year, apples are dipped in honey and a wish is made for a sweet year. Apples and honey come together to create this luscious cake.

Ingredients (for a 26 cm/10 inch diameter springform pan)

The Apple Topping:

2 tablespoons oil
80 g (3 oz, 1/3 cup) light brown sugar
3 tart baking apples, peeled, cored and sliced into 1/2 cm (1/4 inch) slices

The Cake:

3 eggs
180 g (, 61/2 oz, 3/4 cup) dark brown sugar
180 ml (61/2 fl oz, 3/4 cup) oil
250 g (9 oz, 3/4 cup) honey
180 ml (61/2 fl oz, 3/4 cup) apple juice, warm
340 g (12 oz, 21/3 cup) flour
1 teaspoon baking powder
1 teaspoon baking soda
1 teaspoon ground cinnamon
1 teaspoon ground cloves

1. Preheat oven to 180°C (350°F).
2. **Prepare the topping:** Cover the bottom and walls of the pan with the oil. Sprinkle on a uniform coating of the light brown sugar. Arrange apples in one dense layer.
3. **Prepare the cake:** Beat the eggs with the dark brown sugar for 5 minutes until light and fluffy. Add oil and honey and beat until smooth. Add the warm apple juice and mix well.
4. In a separate bowl whisk the flour with the baking powder, baking soda, cinnamon and cloves. Add to the eggs and honey batter and mix until just combined.
5. Bake for 50-55 minutes, until a toothpick comes out dry with a few crumbs adhering. Cool in the pan for 15 minutes. Invert the pan over a large flat serving plate, release the spring and gently lift off the ring. Serve at room temperature.

Pomegranate Granita

Pleasantly tangy and extremely refreshing, pomegranate juice is a great starting point for beverages and desserts. If you can't find pomegranate juice in the stores, you can easily make your own with a citrus juicer. This recipe doesn't call for sugar, but don't worry, grenadine syrup is plenty sweet.

Ingredients (serves 10)
4 cups pomegranate juice
1/3 cup grenadine (pomegranate syrup)
2-3 tablespoons freshly squeezed lemon juice
1-2 tablespoons pomegranate concentrate (optional)
A few drops rose essence (optional)
1/2 cup pomegranate seeds for garnish

1. Whisk all the ingredients together except the pomegranate seeds. The mixture will be both acidic and very sweet but will lose some of its sweetness when frozen.
2. Pour into a large shallow tray, cover and put in the freezer for 2 hours, stirring occasionally. Freeze until firm, 8 to 24 hours.
3. When ready to serve, scrape the granita with a fork to create a crumbly texture, put in glasses or bowls and top with pomegranate seeds.

Figs Confit in Crème de Cassis

Fresh figs are irresistible: sexy, luscious and honey sweet. This recipe will enable you to enjoy this lovely fruit all year long. Serve the confit with a dollop of crème fraîche, thick yogurt or vanilla ice cream. It also goes well with ripe cheese or liver pâté.

Ingredients (makes 1 liter/quart jar)
1 kg (2 lbs 4 oz) fresh firm figs
2 tablespoons freshly squeezed lemon juice
1 kg (2 lbs 4 oz) sugar
11/3 cups Crème de Cassis (or other cassis liqueur)

1. Wash the figs carefully, taking care not to tear the skin. Using a small sharp knife, make 2 slits along each fig about 2 cm (1 inch) long.
2. Transfer the figs to a glass bowl, cover with water mixed with lemon juice, and place an inverted plate on top to make sure they are immersed in the water. Soak overnight.
3. Carefully pat the figs dry with a paper towel and set aside.
4. Bring the sugar and 2 cups of water to a boil in a wide pan. Lower the heat and cook until all the sugar dissolves. Add one cup of the liqueur and carefully arrange the figs on the bottom of the pan. Bring to a boil again and lower the heat to minimum and cook partly covered for about 2 hours. Turn the figs once or twice using a wooden spoon. By the end of the cooking cycle the figs should be translucent. Transfer the fruit to a sterilized jar. Bring the remaining liqueur to a boil and cook on high heat for 20 minutes.
5. Pour the boiling liquid over the figs and add the remaining 1/3 cup of the Crème de Cassis.
6. Seal the jar and store in a cool dark place. The figs will keep for 6 months.

Citrus Semolina Cake

Semolina cakes are found throughout the Middle East and are popular in Jewish Sephardic kitchens. Called basbousa, safra, tishpishti or revani, they can be filled with dates, garnished with almonds, and can even be made with ground walnuts instead of, or in addition to, semolina. These crumbly dry cakes are doused with syrup immediately after baking, making them moist and very sweet.

The following is a slightly unorthodox version that contains freshly squeezed orange (or tangerine) juice and citrus marmalade, and is prepared with separated eggs for a light fluffy texture.

Ingredients (for a 25×30 cm/10×12 inch baking pan)

6 eggs, separated
100 g (3 1/2 oz, 1/2 cup) sugar
100 g (3 1/2 oz, 1 cup) ground coconut
140 g (5 oz, 1 cup) sifted flour
270 g (10 oz, 2 1/2 cups) semolina
25 g (1 oz, 1 1/2 tablespoons) ground almonds
20 g (2 small sachets, 4 teaspoons) baking powder
240 ml (8 1/2 fl oz, 1 cup) oil
360 ml (13 fl oz, 1 1/2 cup) freshly squeezed orange or tangerine juice
2 teaspoons grated orange zest
240 ml (8 1/2 fl oz, 1 cup) orange or lemon marmalade

The Syrup:
1 cup sugar
1 cup water

The Garnish:
Crushed almonds or coconut flakes

1. Preheat the oven to 180°C (350°F).
2. Using an electric mixer beat the egg whites with the sugar for 8 minutes until they hold stiff peaks.
3. Combine all the dry ingredients in a bowl: coconut, flour, semolina, ground almonds and baking powder.
4. Beat the egg yolks in a separate bowl, gradually adding the oil, juice, orange zest and marmalade.
5. Stir in the dry ingredients slowly until combined well. Gently fold in the peaked egg whites.
6. Pour the batter into a well-greased pan and bake for 30 minutes, until the cake turns golden and a toothpick comes out dry with a few crumbs adhering.
7. While the cake is in the oven prepare the syrup: Bring the water and sugar to a boil and simmer for 20 minutes. Cool slightly.
8. Take the cake out of the oven and pour on the syrup evenly. Cool completely and garnish with almonds or coconut.

Cheesecake with Assorted Nuts

Pitsuchim is the collective name for a variety of nuts and seeds consumed in front of the TV or during football matches. In this recipe they add a crunchy twist to another local favorite: the cheesecake traditionally served at the early summer festival of Shavuot.

Ingredients (for a 24 cm/9 inch diameter springform pan)

The Base:
150 g (5 1/2 oz) white chocolate, chopped
150 g (5 1/2 oz, 2 1/4 cups) cornflakes, crushed
125 g (4 1/2 oz) peanut butter

The Cake:
750 g (1 1/2 lbs) *gvina levana* (fresh soft white cheese — see explanation below)
200 ml (7 fl oz) sour cream
120 g (4 oz) confectioners' sugar
14 g (1 sachet, 1/2 oz) gelatin diluted in 1/3 cup boiling water
250 ml (9 fl oz, 1 cup) whipping cream

The Nut and Honey Topping:
25 g (1 oz) butter
1 heaping tablespoon honey
1 tablespoon sugar
1/2 cup cashew nuts
1/2 cup pine nuts (or blanched peanuts)
1/2 cup blanched halved almonds

1. **Prepare the base:** Melt the chocolate in a microwave oven or on a bain-marie (double boiler). Add cornflakes and peanut butter and mix thoroughly. Press firmly onto the bottom of the baking pan lined with baking paper. Put in the freezer.
2. **Prepare the cake:** Combine cheese, sour cream, sugar and gelatin and mix thoroughly.
3. Beat the whipping cream and fold into the cheese mixture. Pour over the base, cover with cling film and refrigerate for 24 hours.
4. **Prepare the topping:** Melt the butter with honey and sugar in a large skillet over medium heat. Add the cashew nuts and stir-fry for 1-2 minutes. Add the pine nuts and almonds and stir-fry for 2 more minutes until golden. Remove from the stove and flatten the nuts on a sheet of baking paper. Cool completely and break into small pieces. Just before serving, remove the cake from the fridge and sprinkle with the nut mixture.

Gvina Levana Literally "white cheese", this soft, fresh, creamy cheese made from cow's milk is similar to German *quark*. It was brought to Palestine by German Templer settlers at the beginning of the 20th Century. In today's Israel it is one of the most popular breakfast foods and is widely used for baking. *Gvina levana* is responsible for the exceptionally light texture and fresh taste of local cheesecakes. Outside Israel, it is sold in Kosher stores carrying fresh Israeli products.

If unavailable, substitute with 500 g (1 lb 2 oz) cream cheese mixed with 250 ml (9 fl oz) sour cream. The cake will be creamier and richer, but equally delicious.

Watermelon Ice in a Chilled Fruit Soup

A perfect treat for a sultry summer day, which we have plenty of in Israel.

Ingredients (serves 4-6)
3 cups watermelon cubes
1/2 cup passion fruit juice (unstrained)
1/2 cup freshly squeezed orange juice
1 cup peach, puréed
1 cup mango, puréed
1/2 cup sugar
3 heaping teaspoons corn starch
To Serve:
1/4 cup assorted berries

1. **Prepare the watermelon ice:** Purée the watermelon in a food processor or with a stick blender. Pass through a fine sieve and pour into an ice cube tray. Freeze overnight.
2. **Prepare the soup:** Bring the ingredients to a simmer, stirring frequently, and cook on low heat until slightly thickened. Chill in the refrigerator (the soup will thicken further).
3. Pour the chilled soup into deep bowls, add 3-4 watermelon cubes to each bowl and garnish with berries.

Ma'amoul —
Date-filled Cookies

These dainty pastries are served with tea or coffee throughout the Middle East. The filling is made with pitted pressed dates, called *ajwa* in Arabic. They are sold in Middle Eastern food stores and markets. If unavailable, pit dried dates and chop them in a food processor (you may need to add a bit of oil). The characteristic grooved pattern is created by a special ma'amoul utensil that looks like a tweezer, but you can get a similar effect with a fork.

Ingredients (for about 50 cookies)
The Filling:
500 g (1 lb 2 oz) pressed pitted dates (see explanation above)
1 teaspoon cinnamon
5 drops orange blossom water
200 g (7 oz) butter, softened
The Dough:
560 g (1 lb 4 oz, 4 cups) bread flour
100 g (31/2 oz, 1 cup) semolina
10 g (1 small sachet, 2 teaspoons) baking powder
1 teaspoon vanilla extract
200 g (7 oz) butter
120 ml (4 oz, 1/2 cup) oil
50 g (2 oz, 1/4 cup) sugar
5 drops orange blossom water
Confectioners' sugar for dusting

1. Preheat the oven to 180°C (350°F).
2. **Prepare the filling:** Combine all the ingredients and mix thoroughly. Roll about fifty balls the size of large olives.
3. **Prepare the dough:** Fit a mixer with a dough hook and knead the ingredients for about 3 minutes to a smooth dough.
4. **Prepare the cookies:** Pinch small pieces off the dough and roll balls twice the size of the date balls. Flatten the ball on the palm of your hand. Place a date ball in the center and reshape into a ball. Create grooves with a special utensil or a fork.
5. Arrange the cookies on a tray lined with baking paper, spacing them, and bake for 20 minutes. Remove from the oven before the cookies turn golden.
6. Dust with confectioners' sugar while the cookies are still warm (the sugar will adhere better), cool and store in an airtight jar.

Tahini and Oatmeal Cookies

Tahini cookies, often called halva cookies (sweetened tahini is in fact halva), are very popular in Israel and prepared in a variety of ways. This recipe shows how tahini can enhance a traditional American oatmeal cookie.

Ingredients (makes 45 cookies)
120 ml (4 oz, 1/2 cup) raw tahini
4 tablespoons butter, softened
140 g (5 oz, 2/3 cup) sugar
1 egg
1 egg white
200 g (7 oz, 2 cups) rolled oats
70 g (21/2 oz, 1/2 cup) whole wheat flour
70 g (21/2 oz, 1/2 cup) self-raising flour
1 cup dried cranberries or raisins
1/2 cup chopped walnuts

1. Preheat oven to 180°C (350°F).
2. Beat tahini, butter, sugar, egg and egg white until smooth and fluffy.
3. Mix the two kinds of flour and gradually beat them into the tahini mixture. Stir in the cranberries and walnuts. Drop batter by tablespoonfuls onto baking sheets lined with baking paper, spacing them.
4. Bake 10 minutes for cookies with soft insides and 15 minutes for hard crispy ones. Do not touch the cookies before they cool completely or they will crumble.

Tahini Ice Cream

Sound weird? Wait till you taste it. A special bonus: you don't need an ice cream machine to make it. Condensed milk will thicken the mixture and help achieve the creamy texture.

Ingredients (makes 1 liter/quart ice cream)
500 ml (1/2 quart, 2 cups) whipping cream
1 can (400 g, 14 oz) sweetened
condensed milk
1/3 cup raw tahini
A dash of ground cinnamon and/or ground
cardamom (optional)
To serve:
1/2 cup halva strands or crumbled halva

1. Beat the cream until soft peaks form. Fold in the condensed milk and the tahini.
2. Freeze in a large bowl or in individual serving cups or goblets.
3. Sprinkle with halva threads or crumbled halva before serving.

Tip If you have an ice cream machine, try adding raw tahini to your favorite vanilla ice cream recipe: about 1/4 cup raw tahini to 2 cups ice cream mixture.

Apple and Calvados Coffee Cake

Large chunks of apples are sautéed in butter, doused with apple brandy, and mixed with fluffy batter and a handful of nuts for crunch. This is one of the best apple cakes you ever tasted.

Ingredients (for a 22 cm/8 inch diameter springform pan or 26cm/10 inch kugelhopf pan)

50 g (2 oz) butter
750 g (11/2 lb) tart baking apples, peeled, cored and cut into 8 wedges each
200 g (7 oz, 1 cup) sugar
3 tablespoons calvados (or brandy)
3 eggs
140 g (5 oz, 1 cup) flour
1 teaspoon baking powder
1 teaspoon cinnamon
120 ml (4 fl oz, 1/2 cup) oil
50 g (2 oz, 1/2 cup) walnuts, coarsely chopped

1. Melt butter in a large skillet. Add apples and sauté on low heat until tender but firm, about 10 minutes. Add 1/4 cup sugar and calvados, cook for one minute and remove from stove. Let cool.
2. Preheat oven to 170°C (325°F).
3. Beat the eggs with the remaining 3/4 cup sugar at high speed until fluffy and airy, about 10 minutes.
4. Sift the flour with the baking powder and cinnamon. Lower the speed of the mixer and gradually add the flour and the oil. Fold in the apples and the nuts.
5. Pour the batter into a well-greased baking pan. Bake for 45 minutes, until the cake is golden brown. Serve at room temperature.

Malabi Sampler

Originally sold from street carts in disposable goblets, this snow white, fluttering, perfumed pudding is now featured on every trendy restaurant menu. Once you master the basic recipe you can create a host of delicious and beautiful desserts.

Ingredients (for 12 servings in half-cup goblets)

4 cups (1 liter, 1 quart) milk
75 g (3 oz, 3/4 cup) corn starch
1 tablespoon rose water or 2-3 drops rose essence
240 ml (81/2 fl oz, 1 cup) whipping cream
100 g (31/2 oz, 1/2 cup) sugar
To Serve:
Raspberry syrup with rose water to taste
Coarsely chopped roasted pistachio nuts
Coconut flakes

1. In a bowl, mix one cup of milk with the corn starch and rose water until the corn starch dissolves completely.
2. Bring the remaining milk together with the whipping cream and sugar to a simmer. Pour in the dissolved corn starch mixture and cook 2-3 minutes over low heat, stirring constantly, until the mixture thickens.
3. Remove from the stove and pour into serving dishes. Cover with cling wrap, allow to cool to room temperature, and refrigerate for at least 4 hours.
4. Serve with raspberry syrup perfumed with rose water and garnish with chopped pistachio nuts and/or coconut flakes.

More Options Basic malabi is neutral in taste, so let your imagination run wild and create enticing desserts using various toppings and garnishes: berries, sliced or diced fresh fruit, fruit preserves, pomegranate seeds, candied citrus peels, etc.

Malabi Trifle Prepare the malabi as described and pour into a large round-bottomed bowl. Cool and refrigerate. To serve, pry loose and turn over into a large deep serving dish. Garnish with syrup or any of the above toppings.

Malabi "Shots" Refrigerate the pudding in shot glasses and serve two or three "shots" per guest, each one with a different topping.

Passover Chocolate and Nut Cake

Baking without flour is quite a challenge, but it often produces absolutely delectable cakes and pastries. This one is brimming with goodies: nuts, chocolate, coconut and dried apricots. A silicone pan is especially convenient for baking this crumbly cake.

Ingredients (for a 24 cm/9 inch kugelhopf pan, preferably silicone)
6 tablespoons sugar
6 eggs
6 tablespoons matzo meal
6 tablespoons oil
150 g (5 1/2 oz) coconut
150 g (5 1/2 oz) walnuts, chopped finely
150 g (5 1/2 oz) bittersweet chocolate, chopped finely
100 g (3 1/2 oz) dried apricots, chopped finely
Confectioners' sugar for dusting

1. Preheat oven to 180°C (350°F).
2. Beat eggs and sugar at high speed for 8 minutes until airy and fluffy.
3. Mix matzo meal with oil, coconut, nuts, chocolate and dried apricots. Fold in about one-quarter of the beaten eggs at a time.
4. Pour the batter into a greased pan and bake for 35 minutes, until a toothpick comes out dry with a few crumbs adhering. Cool and dust with confectioners' sugar before serving. The cake will keep for 4 days.

Recipe Index